POEMS BY
LEWIS CARROLL

XA[illegible]
MA[illegible]
MICHELLE [illegible]AUX
[illegible]MITH

JABBERWOCKY
AND OTHER POEMS

Contents

OXFORD
UNIVERSITY PRESS

Jabberwocky

’Twas brillig, and the slithy toves
Did gyre and gimble in the wabe;
All mimsy were the borogoves,
And the mome raths outgrabe.

Beware the Jabberwock, my son!
The jaws that bite, the claws that catch!
Beware the Jubjub bird and shun
The frumious Bandersnatch!

He took his vorpal sword in hand:

Long time the manxome foe he sought—

So rested he by the Tumtum tree,
And stood awhile in thought.

And as in uffish thought he stood,
  The Jabberwock, with eyes of flame,
Came whiffling through the tulgey wood,
  And burbled as it came!

One, two! One, two! And through and through
The vorpal blade went snicker-snack!
SNICKER-SNACK!
Ahh!

Urggghhhhh!
He left it dead, and with its head
He went galumphing back.

And hast thou slain the Jabberwock?
Come to my arms, my beamish boy!
O frabjous day!
Callooh! Callay!
He chortled in his joy.

’Twas brillig, and the slithy toves
Did gyre and gimble in the wabe;
All mimsy were the borogoves,
And the mome raths outgrabe.

Jabberwocky

'Twas brillig, and the slithy toves
  Did gyre and gimble in the wabe;
All mimsy were the borogoves,
  And the mome raths outgrabe.

'Beware the Jabberwock, my son!
  The jaws that bite, the claws that catch!
Beware the Jubjub bird and shun
  The frumious Bandersnatch!'

He took his vorpal sword in hand:
  Long time the manxome foe he sought—
So rested he by the Tumtum tree,
  And stood awhile in thought.

And as in uffish thought he stood,
  The Jabberwock, with eyes of flame,
Came whiffling through the tulgey wood,
  And burbled as it came!

One, two! One, two! And through and through
  The vorpal blade went snicker-snack!
He left it dead, and with its head
  He went galumphing back.

'And hast thou slain the Jabberwock?
  Come to my arms, my beamish boy!
O frabjous day! Callooh! Callay!'
  He chortled in his joy.

'Twas brillig, and the slithy toves
  Did gyre and gimble in the wabe;
All mimsy were the borogoves,
  And the mome raths outgrabe.

How Doth the Little Crocodile

How doth the little crocodile
Improve his shining tail,
And pour the waters of the Nile
On every golden scale!

How cheerfully he seems to grin,
How neatly spreads his claws,
And welcomes little fishes in
With gently smiling jaws!

The Walrus and the Carpenter

The sea was wet as wet could be,
  The sands were dry as dry.
You could not see a cloud, because
  No cloud was in the sky:
No birds were flying overhead—
  There were no birds to fly.

The Walrus and the Carpenter
  Were walking close at hand;
They wept like anything to see
  Such quantities of sand;
'If this were only cleared away,'
  They said, 'it *would* be grand!'

'If seven maids with seven mops
Swept it for half a year,
Do you suppose,' the Walrus said,
'That they could get it clear?'
'I doubt it,' said the Carpenter,
And shed a bitter tear.
June
May
March
'O Oysters, come and walk with us!'
The Walrus did beseech.
'A pleasant walk, a pleasant talk,
Along the briny beach:
We cannot do with more than four,
To give a hand to each.'

The eldest Oyster looked at him,
But never a word he said:
The eldest Oyster winked his eye,
And shook his heavy head—
Meaning to say he did not choose
To leave the oyster-bed.
But four young Oysters hurried up,
All eager for the treat:
Their coats were brushed, their faces washed,
Their shoes were clean and neat—
And this was odd, because, you know,
They hadn't any feet.

Four other Oysters followed them,
  And yet another four;
And thick and fast they came at last,
  And more, and more, and more—
All hopping through the frothy waves,
  And scrambling to the shore.

The Walrus and the Carpenter
  Walked on a mile or so,
And then they rested on a rock
  Conveniently low:
And all the little Oysters stood
  And waited in a row.

'The time has come,' the Walrus said,
'To talk of many things:
Of shoes—and ships—and sealing wax—
Of cabbages—and kings—
And why the sea is boiling hot—
And whether pigs have wings.'

'But wait a bit,' the Oysters cried,
'Before we have our chat;
For some of us are out of breath,
And all of us are fat!'
'No hurry!' said the Carpenter.
They thanked him much for that.

'A loaf of bread,' the Walrus said,
'Is what we chiefly need;
Pepper and vinegar besides
Are very good indeed—
Now, if you're ready, Oysters dear,
We can begin to feed.'
'But not on us,' the Oysters cried,
Turning a little blue.
'After such kindness that would be
A dismal thing to do!'
'The night is fine,' the Walrus said,
'Do you admire the view?'

'It was so kind of you to come,
  And you are very nice!'
The Carpenter said nothing but,
  'Cut us another slice.
I wish you were not quite so deaf—
  I've had to ask you twice!'

'It seems a shame,' the Walrus said,
  'To play them such a trick.
After we've brought them out so far
  And made them trot so quick!'
The Carpenter said nothing but,
  'The butter's spread too thick!'

‘I weep for you,’ the Walrus said,
‘I deeply sympathize.’
With sobs and tears he sorted out
Those of the largest size,
Holding his pocket-handkerchief
Before his streaming eyes.

‘O Oysters,’ said the Carpenter,
‘You’ve had a pleasant run!
Shall we be trotting home again?’
But answer came there none—
And this was scarcely odd, because
They’d eaten every one.’

The Walrus and the Carpenter

The sun was shining on the sea,
Shining with all his might:
He did his very best to make
The billows smooth and bright—
And this was odd, because it was
The middle of the night.

The moon was shining sulkily,
Because she thought the sun
Had got no business to be there
After the day was done—
'It's very rude of him,' she said,
'To come and spoil the fun!'

The sea was wet as wet could be,
The sands were dry as dry.
You could not see a cloud, because
No cloud was in the sky:
No birds were flying overhead—
There were no birds to fly.

The Walrus and the Carpenter
Were walking close at hand;
They wept like anything to see
Such quantities of sand;
'If this were only cleared away,'
They said, 'it *would* be grand!'

'If seven maids with seven mops
Swept it for half a year,
Do you suppose,' the Walrus said,
'That they could get it clear?'
'I doubt it,' said the Carpenter,
And shed a bitter tear.

'O Oysters, come and walk with us!'
  The Walrus did beseech.
'A pleasant walk, a pleasant talk,
  Along the briny beach:
We cannot do with more than four,
  To give a hand to each.'

The eldest Oyster looked at him,
  But never a word he said:
The eldest Oyster winked his eye,
  And shook his heavy head—
Meaning to say he did not choose
  To leave the oyster-bed.

But four young Oysters hurried up,
  All eager for the treat:
Their coats were brushed, their faces washed,
  Their shoes were clean and neat—
And this was odd, because, you know,
  They hadn't any feet.

Four other Oysters followed them,
  And yet another four;
And thick and fast they came at last,
  And more, and more, and more—
All hopping through the frothy waves,
  And scrambling to the shore.

The Walrus and the Carpenter
  Walked on a mile or so,
And then they rested on a rock
  Conveniently low:
And all the little Oysters stood
  And waited in a row.

'The time has come,' the Walrus said,
'To talk of many things:
Of shoes—and ships—and sealing wax—
Of cabbages—and kings—
And why the sea is boiling hot—
And whether pigs have wings.'

'But wait a bit,' the Oysters cried,
'Before we have our chat;
For some of us are out of breath,
And all of us are fat!'
'No hurry!' said the Carpenter.
They thanked him much for that.

'A loaf of bread,' the Walrus said,
'Is what we chiefly need;
Pepper and vinegar besides
Are very good indeed—
Now, if you're ready, Oysters dear,
We can begin to feed.'

'But not on us,' the Oysters cried,
Turning a little blue.
'After such kindness that would be
A dismal thing to do!'
'The night is fine,' the Walrus said,
'Do you admire the view?'

'It was so kind of you to come,
  And you are very nice!'
The Carpenter said nothing but,
  'Cut us another slice.
I wish you were not quite so deaf—
  I've had to ask you twice!'

'It seems a shame,' the Walrus said,
  'To play them such a trick.
After we've brought them out so far
  And made them trot so quick!'
The Carpenter said nothing but,
  'The butter's spread too thick!'

'I weep for you,' the Walrus said,
  'I deeply sympathize.'
With sobs and tears he sorted out
  Those of the largest size,
Holding his pocket-handkerchief
  Before his streaming eyes.

'O Oysters,' said the Carpenter,
  'You've had a pleasant run!
Shall we be trotting home again?'
  But answer came there none—
And this was scarcely odd, because
  They'd eaten every one.

Humpty Dumpty's Recitation

In winter, when the fields are white,
I sing this song for your delight—

In spring, when woods are getting green,
I'll try and tell you what I mean.

In summer, when the days are long,
Perhaps you'll understand the song.

In autumn, when the leaves are brown,
Take pen and ink and write it down.

I sent a message to the fish:
I told them 'This is what I wish.'
The little fishes of the sea
They sent an answer back to me.
The little fishes' answer was
'We cannot do it, Sir, because—'

I sent to them again to say
'It will be better to obey.'
The fishes answered with a grin,
'Why, what a temper you are in!'
I told them once, I told them twice:
They would not listen to advice.

I took a kettle large and new,
Fit for the deed I had to do.
My heart went hop, my heart went thump;
I filled the kettle at the pump.
Then someone came to me and said
'The little fishes are in bed.'
ZZZZZZZZZZZZZZZZ

I said to him, I said it plain,
'Then you must wake them up again.'
I said it loud and very clear;
I went and shouted in his ear.
But he was very stiff and proud;
He said 'You needn't shout so loud!'

And he was very proud and stiff;
He said 'I'll go and wake them, if—'

I took a corkscrew from the shelf:
I went to wake them up myself.

And when I found the door was locked,
I pulled and pushed and kicked and knocked.
And when I found the door was shut,
I tried to turn the handle, but—

Humpty Dumpty's Recitation

In winter, when the fields are white,
I sing this song for your delight—

In spring, when woods are getting green,
I'll try and tell you what I mean.

In summer, when the days are long,
Perhaps you'll understand the song.

In autumn, when the leaves are brown,
Take pen and ink and write it down.

I sent a message to the fish:
I told them 'This is what I wish.'

The little fishes of the sea
They sent an answer back to me.

The little fishes' answer was
'We cannot do it, Sir, because—'

I sent to them again to say
'It will be better to obey.'

The fishes answered with a grin,
'Why, what a temper you are in!'

I told them once, I told them twice:
They would not listen to advice.

I took a kettle large and new,
Fit for the deed I had to do.

My heart went hop, my heart went thump;
I filled the kettle at the pump.

Then some one came to me and said
'The little fishes are in bed.'

I said to him, I said it plain,
'Then you must wake them up again.'

I said it loud and very clear;
I went and shouted in his ear.

But he was very stiff and proud;
He said 'You needn't shout so loud!'

And he was very proud and stiff;
He said 'I'll go and wake them, if—'

I took a corkscrew from the shelf:
I went to wake them up myself.

And when I found the door was locked,
I pulled and pushed and kicked and knocked.

And when I found the door was shut,
I tried to turn the handle, but—

About Lewis Carroll

Lewis Carroll's real name was Charles Lutwidge Dodgson. He was born on 27th January 1832, in Cheshire, England. He was the eldest boy in his family, with three brothers and six sisters. He was very shy and tended to stammer when he spoke.

Lewis did well at school and went on to study at Christ Church, Oxford University. He stayed on at the university to work in mathematics. It was there he got to know the children of the Dean (the head of the college) – Alice Liddell and her two sisters.

He often made up stories for the girls. Once, on a boat trip, Lewis told a particularly long and strange story about Alice. She asked him to write it down for her, and when it was finished, an author they knew recommended getting it published. This story became *Alice's Adventures in Wonderland.* It was published in 1865 and soon became the most popular children's book in England.

As well as being a writer and mathematician, Lewis was an accomplished photographer, but today he is mainly remembered for *Alice's Adventures in Wonderland* and its sequel, *Through the Looking-Glass*, published in 1872.

Lewis died in January 1898, in Guildford, England.